W9-AGE-492

the Gift of an Angel

for parents
welcoming a new child

Written and Illustrated by
Marianne Richmond

The Gift of an Angel

is dedicated

to Jim who knows all the reasons why – MR

Published by Mare Rich Studios

420 North Fifth Street, #840, Minneapolis, MN 55401

http://www.marerich.com

1 (800) 768-9197

Printed and bound in the United States of America

ISBN 0-9652448-0-6

Illustrations by Marianne Richmond

Book design by Lecy Design

Gentle color erased night's shadows.

Warm breezes nudged the world awake.

Bees and butterflies began to play,

as sunshine kissed the lake.

A midst all this earthly ardor,

heaven stirred with anticipation,

and God tended to the final touch

of His miracle of creation.

Gathering His host of angels,

the Lord considered them one by one.

"I need a volunteer," He said,

"to watch over this daughter or son."

"I've created a child so unique

yet so needy of guidance and care.

I want to insure that an angel

will for this child be there."

Then a beautiful angel with demeanor

always gentle, always mild,

accepted the Lord's invitation

to be guardian of the child.

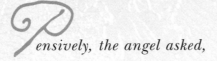*ensively, the angel asked,*

"For this family, what can I do?

Aren't the parents you've chosen capable?

Won't they watch this child for you?"

"They will, my angel," said the Lord.

"But they can't be everywhere.

That's why I wish to give to them

my constant loving care.

"Your role in the child's life,

will gently unfold with the days.

You'll be a protector, keeper, friend . . .

and wise teacher of life's ways.

"You'll inspire the child to explore

as only a little child can,

with wide-eyed wonder and innocence

with impulsive abandon.

"*You'll nudge your child to open*

the door to where dreams can run free—

a world where the curious spirit

plays with fun and spontaneity.

"*A place where a child can play pretend*

with pirates, fairies and kings,

living on high seas and in strong castles

orchestrating awesome, imaginative things.

"*And you'll lead the child down paths*

filled with wonders of everyday—

a pudgy caterpillar, a plump bumblebee,

a butterfly meandering her way.

"*You'll bestow on this family the wonder*

that lets parents see through child's eyes,

helping them recapture the innocence

and moments of sweet surprise.

"*Through you, they'll know heaven's goodness,*

gentle peace that comes with love.

Days will be radiant and nights be filled

with quiet harmony from above."

Then the angel teetered on heaven's edge,

peering down on a waiting earth.

For a brief moment all time stood still

just moments before the birth.

"One more thing, dear angel, before you go,"

said the Lord to His chosen one.

"Life is not always laughter and smiles . . .

not all discovery and fun.

"There will be frightening times for sure

when danger stirs alarm.

It's then you must forget all else

and protect this child from harm."

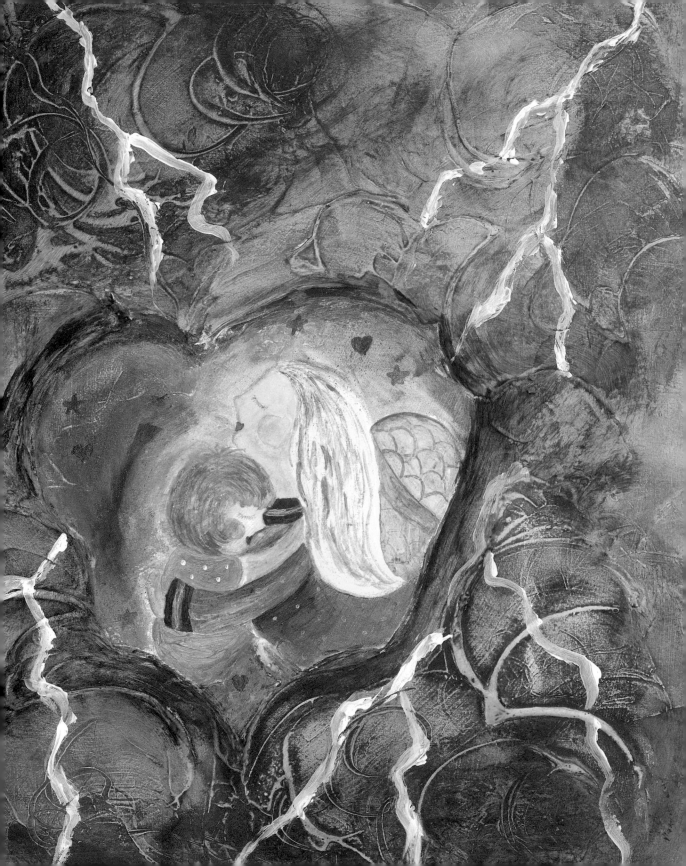

"I understand," the angel said,

"the importance of this lifelong task.

Be assured for counsel and guidance

on you I'll call and ask."

And so it was at heaven's door

as the angel prepared for flight

that God said, "Be good and do your best,"

and hugged His angel tight.

With that, the angel grabbed a star

    and tumbled from on high,

touching down as earth resounded

    with a baby's sweet, pure cry.

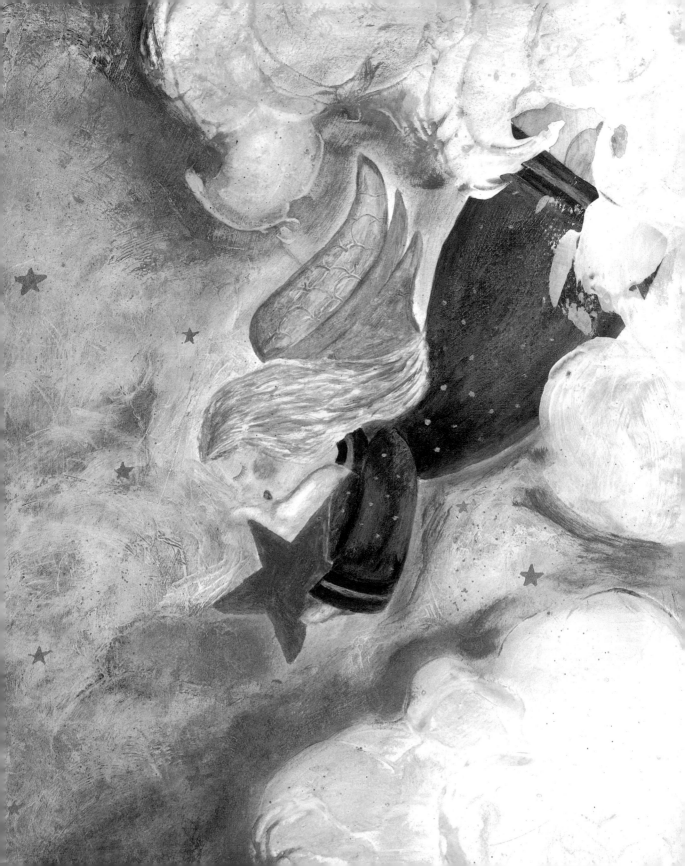

At precisely 7:02AM *on* October 3, 1998

heaven's angel witnessed the birth

of Luke Richard Dennen

God's newest blessing on earth.

Marianne Richmond

*Artist and writer Marianne Richmond shares her work
with hundreds of thousands of people every year through the
greeting card company she owns with her husband, Jim.
Her cards, sold under the Watercolor Works name,
can be found around the country and in Canada.*
The Gift of an Angel *is Marianne's first book. "I have many
angels in my life…people who inspire, teach and care about
me." said Marianne. "This book is a gift to parents, a chance
to believe in one of the first angels in their child's life."*